Copyright © 2025 Ніка Мавроди
You may quote from but not recycle this book.
Back cover includes art by Jamieson W. Cash

AF110154

979-8-3492-4954-9

Çé dill

sobriety versus straight-edge

loofah never turned up mold like refrigerated cabbage, but Healthline alarms: "sponges aren't necessarily dangerous, but they need to be." Remind me how one party got associated with post-European inclusivity to say Abraham Lincoln's emancipation proclamation was another act of hypocrisy, though now it's fashionable to cast doctors after Hippocrates like with Merriam-Webster, stage actors, thanks to Erving Goffman? It was Heather Love who mentioned him in reference to Judith Butler's citing him in the

1988 **Gender Trouble** preview for *Theatre Journal* Vol. 40, No. 4, pp. 519-531 as if otherwise: Love "interprets Goffman's theory as 'in' my theory, but does not say that I read or used his theory" Butler consented in an email dated 1 September 2022. Those people are employed by universities to assume the duties of faculty, but in Goffman's work — as Butler prints — there's "a self which assumes and exchanges various 'roles.'" What harmony evinces conviviality/connivance between Alice Goffman's father and his friend, winner of the First Erving Goffman Prize Pierre Bourdieu, must be bilingual. Even his 1996 work "on television," translated by the Priscilla Parkhurst Ferguson whose nephew is an attorney in Minneapolis, Bourdieu doesn't bother to comment on performance referring to public individuals by the euphemism Agent that Professor Ferguson renders as Actor for anglophone readers, as his neologism habitus essentializes institutionalization; whether the profession is a natural or social fact occupies academic tongues instead of publics. And cabbage used to grow like flowers at the sides of gorgeous skyscrapers on Lake Shore Drive towards Michigan Avenue.

Presentation of Self in Everyday Life substantiates Renaissance views on how the world's a stage with players while the subsequent *Asylums: Essays on the Social Situation of Mental Patients and Other Inmates* belabors the paradigm, implying hospitalization akin to "destiny" (p. 145) for "the person seeking a robe and audience before which to cower" (169). If linguistic economy belongs to poets, oughn't we ask why the professor mentioned the boarding school but not his university campus in theorizing the total institution by noticing reciprocity as "destination" (9) between patients and {psychiatric} clinicians given how "Each party to the relationship is destined to seek out the other to offer what the other cannot accept, and each is destined to reject what the other offers" (368). Goffman's monograph itemizes field work at National Institute of Mental Health in **Beth**esda, Maryland and the proximate St. Elizabeths Psychiatric Hospital; the conclusion's conformity with Freudianism prompts close-reading on motive. The paper workshopping Asylums shortly before publication says mental patients "suffer" but "not from mental illness." Actually my question is what Erving Goffman traded his sanity for when he left his fieldwork, Frankenstein? (Elizabeth is the affianced heroine of Mary Wollstonecraft Shelley's debut.) Her lede became framed in the epistolary threads of Percy's republicanism, but I remember it verbatim thanks to Anne Mellor and Charles E. Robinson: "servants had any request to make, it was always through her." Can that be? Sortly. Bodelian's line-break finds me there; the editor "supplied a missing word <was> to complete sense" (256n1). Representing a prosperous household, from the servant class Mary figures only Justine Moritz whose confession hastens both Elizabeth and herself dying. Prosthesis goes to her set piece, literary history's first zombie. Colonialism surfaced Haitian religion for an object of fascination in European societies, where priests chemically simulate death as psychiatric alternative to incarceration. Toussaint Louverture's celebrity fused with scientific discourse known to Frankenstein experts as British galvanism or what Julia Douthwaite Viglione identifies with *The Frankenstein of 1790*, her recovery of a Palais Royal printing of Felix Nogaret's "Story of Two Faces" wherein his debutante

Aglaonice {"combining the Greek words **agla** (grace) and **nice** (victor)" (73)} screens her sister's fiancé Wak-wik-vauk-on-son-frankénsteïn "Frankénsteïn" herself marrying Nicator, perhaps an Ovidian double, in the process. Douthwaite notices wik would be "pronounced vic (for Victor?)" (77) cementing the pamphlet's relevance to students of Shelley. perhaps an Ovidian double, in the process. Douthwaite notices wik would be "pronounced vic (for Victor?)" (77) cementing the pamphlet's relevance to students of Shelley. Being a creative writer myself toggling between making art with fiction and using nonfiction to communicate, I can attest to the variable facticity in novels, their ilk, and poetry by introducing the idea of anchors. As a suffix, -ship means relation as derived from Anglo-Saxon coasts; whereas JudeoChristian religious texts distance their readers, modern literature attaches via formal entanglement with epistolarity (cf. 'the novel in letters' was the eighteenth-century's bestseller). Following 1821-1880's theory of establishing fictive space using a 'rule of threes' to describe a room by triangulating its objects, imaginaries cohere through referents shared between our likely audience and us (the author). Personally believing the best anchors for 'autonomous' or 'disinterested' art as mandated by modernism are textile/textual, what is not semiotic? In genres like SciFi, for which Frankenstein has been termed urtext, homo sapian embodiment may be its only anchor! Literary exegesis works not by pointing at whatever atavisms or banalities suffuse or anchor creation; it elucidates relevance. My other account regarding Wollstonecraft-Shelley's source (apart from the "waking dream" she joked about in 1831 from a preface whose descriptive details have been corroborated by "a team of astronomers from Texas State University-San Marcos" is University of Reading's explainer on "Mary Wollstonecraft, frankenstein, and the royal humane society." Its historian Carolyn Williams recounts how Ms. Wollstonecraft's rescue from drowning after quitting Sadean Paris was even presciently anticipated by our "female Wert[h]er" (as her second husband remembered his daughter Mary Shelley's mother posthumously) by London's Royal Humane Society, spinning-off from Amsterdam's 1768 philanthropy whose by London's Royal Humane Society, spinning-off from Amsterdam's 1768 philanthropy whose ten directors "included among their number a Johann Goll van Frankenstein." Frankenstein Castle is located near Frankfurt in Germany where Victor Frankenstein took novel ends from Cornelius Agrippa; its medieval inhabitants may have traveled to Holland after hospitality to merchants evading Spanish Inquisition concurrently with English pilgrimage. Sadism's namesake had his Bastille romance Justine published there in 1791 "Chez les Libraires Associés" while Palais-Égalité remained printing under "Chez Desenne, Libraire, au..." Whether Mrs. Shelley could have read an untranslated "Story of Two Faces" and excluded it from her journals, where she tracked their reading merits doubt. Access to Donatien Alphonse's oeuvre was likewise rather scant though her traveling company contained George Byron whose possessing Les Malheurs de la Vertu reportedly coalesced with the dissolation of his marriage on Charlotte Brontë's birthday before his trip to Switzerland with Mary's stepsister. Leslie Merchand's biography quotes from a parliamentary associate's diary on 26 April 1816, when House of Commons printed "The First Annual Report Concerning Madhouses," that The Baroness Wentworth (whose Ada King pioneered computer science) "looked at a trunk in which B. kept his black drop and Justine" (559) according to "the only surviving daughter of John 'Mad Jack' Byron," Ada's grandfather. (Lord Broughton, "Byron's close friend, was familiar with Justine" says page 553 of Will McMorran's "article" for "The Modern Language Review.") So what? Wollstonecraft didn't know him because if so her polemic could have landed feminism instead of "merely" (Ngai) pioneering it; her acquaintance in France was Thomas Paine. Your idea that a sadist text could have ended up in Wollstonecraft-Shelley's Female-Quixotic library is a fiction Edward Said didn't approve of either. Byron carrying or mentioning it to their Villa Diodati party is thus likely, since readers have noticed *Frankenstein* replete with allusions explicitly too. A narratological doppelgänger for her protagonist (Elizabeth) given as Justine Moritz renders the "servant class" which opens her manuscript a double of what will later also be called "the second sex" (Jeffrey Eugenides' gloss over this politics in *The Marriage Plot* is beloved, but rarely cited elsewhere).; the novel's poetry hangs on her melodramatic innocence and execution. Someone else has already identified Frankenstein's patriarch with the Don, whose surname Francois has come to be synonymous with his nation-state. If Shelley's father had been apprised of another literary reputation's rise concordantly with revolutionary France is more probable but unsubstantiated.

I fell in love with their history during my summer in Polynesia, where George Byron's wikipedia page outmatched his *Don Juan* for its gossip on how he attracted attention for snacking on saltines and a novel by a Laureate from South Africa reminded me of my own libretto having been not so derivative or fanatic literarily. At an exam back in California I was asked to comment only about the contemporary literature, so I mentioned the dogs which are so wild on the island no one would mistake them for our friends.

Jamieson Cash

Hôtel for 1

He called after two video selfies dropped, "I broke up with my girlfriend last week." My battery exhausted already blue then he mentioned pregnancy loss. An episodic novel might not individualize suffering, do you? Calculating abortion as a financial biopolitics is someone else's mental illness; I exist a priori language acquisition but not Pierre's *Distinction*. Jamieson W. Cash is sexy but the name trips me. Averring the postwar feminist motif of socialization, his matriarch Nancy gave him her surname like a calling card? His parents met at Catholic school "in Minnesota whose graduates might break news with their obituaries. More of a local though, the couple had their firstborn in Florida before Elizabeth Victoria's birth abroad. She is a blonde whose loveliness could be redacted from this work; otherwise little is known about her character though not whereabouts or associate, whose ID evokes a postbac bloodletting since Kasia Hayden took Bennington from Ariella Miller. The Brat Pack was always mine, actually. That Miller's Marlboro cigarette went out for the transcendentalists in Massachusetts after all Mark Greif had to say about Thoreau ("it's a pond") is only a reflection on her ex-boyfriend's predilection for stalkerish mockery." Do you know Greif? Assuming sans pronouns in the case of an only child whose cosplaying adulthood tires. Their mother wrote a couple papers about socializing children that includes one consideration of the politeness rituals "Hi, thanks, and goodbye" that neglects apology. Sorely an intern his office hired to expense Harvard's brand spun it for a declined invitation (no, regrets) copping **ugly feelings**. At least it was another occasion to read some Emily Gould, whose shine betters unbound.

Some winter after очередном ихамен I found her account of the debate between Donald Trump and Hilary Clinton in New York Magazine's fashion blog as refracted through a view party with her husband and his friend. To paraphrase her, she said "I'd believe a woman." After our meeting with my students that term, she and I both checked in to different psychiatric wards. What's funny is she's a transfer graduate at my college from Kenyon in Ohio which is the surname of Jamieson's ex-girlfriend at Northrup King, Abby — like the epistolary character you may recognize from dailies. Was president Van Buren the one who got stuck in a bathtub? Gould quit her job blogging Gawker before a Girardian came after it with Hulk Hogan. As a feminist on the media vertical her job was to create synergy, literally with Jezebel-dot-com though Nick Denton's stable was a trojan for mainstreaming porn. What must be said about his project is how its embrace of traffic-driven content pronounced literati voice. The security guard at my elementary school Ms Hogan cared for a daughter in my year, Eileen; not that I ever cared for whether Otessa Moshfegh's "paint-by-numbers" debut was pigeon mail! Titled Eileen it was received in every outlet I could have used a conversation with to avoid the tragedy that befell my fa_e and/or she has a mole, writers. My own is a college friend whose purse y'all are the ones with access to while I brew lexicology. Spending all there was was for awaiting returns. During an episode, cents feel like dollars. Not one gives where interest ought to be but where there aren't almost taxes. I can't know whether my diagnosis is a phenomenology! How my 'presentation of self' (Goffman) does or doesn't conform to psychiatric labels is moot without a control: I've read the textbook[s], save yours? Imagine being an alien in this foreign place asked to disclose identity pathologically. No, Aileen Hall is the one who called from Eileen Hogan's school when the television broadcast Mario Garcia's arrest. And I wasn't asked to comment by extracurricular therapists or school officials; someone's casting that as my evil plan from day one as a student in their haze. Dolores taught ballet catty-corner to our haute gossip where they meet bills instead. Anything might happen during childhood, including enrollment #lolita

There could still be a photo uploaded to Facebook from that Saturday in Evanston where Zac and I were paying a call to Yoel. I was fine in skin-thin gray cotton pants like pajamas or loungewear but it was the weekend. He was just starting out as a filmmaker and his equipment was too good for me to compete—otherwise I would have taken that instead of 'sick girl theory' (a crossover from 'sad girl theory' in the annals of close-tab). Was there anything to say? Or just stare out into a question mark for closure. Whatever became of former Soviet President Joseph Stalin's countryperson after his studies with my relation at Oxford Sophocles Mavroeidis Google answers as Cubist by Point72, a euphemism for Under Investigation albeit alluding to the chapel interior and fashion designs of Pable Picasso на юге Франции where two McGill University graduates married via glass-stomping following advanced English degrees. Gregory Cash claims a relation to the French Canadians whose geneology ended in North America according to sources like geni.com but not before they could return to Paris for lending naming to Marie Antoinette or produce one Marc Tessier-Lavigne originally from Montreal now occupying Palo Alto as an entitled neuroscientist with McGill branding framing his office. While Pierre-Esprit Radisson hadn't descendants save heiress Edna Dickerson from Chicago in spirit, francophone fur trader Jean Baptiste Point du Sable had at least two. Remembered as Chicago's founder, he was actually forced out to St. Louis, Missouri, where his corpse has gone MIA. Yesterday evening Jamieson-Cash offered compliments for the chef des affairs whose diplomacy is not qualified enough to be mired in Cold War. My rebuttal was that Donald Trump's election was produced by the Russian wannabe monarchy he charged with being "a left-wing talking point" with me claiming it's journalism. Translation goes that I own square facts in that arena by virtue of the playground Marat Guelman stole from my summer nights with Greta for purporting society with Vanya Засурский on Livejournal, in all seriousness. Their invitations stopped short of the tablecloth Vladimir Putin set for Mr Trump in 2013 after Michael Oger's 2011 wedding to e-Lena Эдуа́рдовна Бояко́ва; weather was not unseasonably chilly that night, but whether gonzo was a style of pornography first can be a historical question: Am I history or its chronicler? Kate Hayles averred to the latter, I lean in towards its former. But then what are you.

President/Precedent :j

It's 1997. Our president effects sexual offense thanks to news media but no one hesitates to place Joanne Rowling's debut fantasy detective series in children's hands though the literary academy is ablaze with New Historicism, which finds discourse silos collapsing not Copernican. Plus an art gallery hosts the launch of an Auckie's **I Love Rich** subculture snuff whereas uptown Vivian Gornick's essay collection salvages the unsalvageable *Art Militaire des Chinois* after Random House made **The Deal** to Trump Minnesota's *Inquiry Into Values* (1974). Plus an art gallery hosts the launch of an Auckie's I Love Rich subculture snuff whereas uptown Vivian Gornick's essay collection salvages the unsalvageable Art Militaire des Chinois after Random House made The Deal to Trump Minnesota's Inquiry Into Values (1974). It's not like university accommodations are public housing—that's the White House. All I wished was for it to be renamed or repainted, perhaps both. But being made to feel having an opinion about domestic affairs is unamerican has been oppressive. Constitutionally banned from holding any office whatsoever, I'm deplatformed also. Maybe for observing a broken system thus blamed out of shame. How was President Obama? Graduated by now. What precedent were you all banking on from him? Not me. Leaving New York City because Manhattan wore they chased out and forced me back using one of those reality stars. It feels like the deportations and televised hate wouldn't happening at this pitch or frequency if I hadn't left the borderland (yes, on some level I was hoping it would be permanent), not that I'm a cause. Irreconcilable paradigms were how your constitution disqualifies me from office while an anglophone feminism mandates conformity to novel virtues I'd like to write. What I'm saying is everywhere but here is a Manhattan I can now never visit: that is, cleaner safer and mobile. Chapo Trap House tropes diapers with the alt-right, nary my bibliography. Bickering about my candidacy was reportedly flamed between Greif and his colleague Mark Algee-Hewitt, a Canadian whose recent presentation on "transremediation" was no less triggering than average. Purportedly 'a nice guy' to those who can afford it (not me) what he instead performs is pettiness. Finding three Marks in a comparatively minor faculty at the deceased Leland Stanford Junior's office of English language and literature spelled idiosyncrasy, having acknowledged morbidity. I hadn't read the New Testament much prior to my repulse nor did anyone responsible for my spiritual upbringing ever indicate its necessity, nor did your laws. "He's an English professor," Bari Weiss announced of her panelist at the online event in 2023, "don't hold that against him." I slept through Andrew Meier's seminar the day of Greif's teaching presentation on Chuck Klosterman. An administrator enrolled me in the title about Jewish intellectuals and "little magazines" in New York City the following term. Arriving to a seated classroom with a lovely view on 11th street, he jotted "Prof. Greif" on the chalkboard backtracking within weeks to a correction of my correspondence only in that I wrote "Hey [Mark]" instead of "Hi is okay" or 'better yet' "Dear." In a phone call with Professor Emerita Nancy Armstrong all these years later, I explained my English was made from being on the playground as charged by Chicago Public Schools thus what wouldn't be imaginable during a Windsor tea totally belong "in my repertoire—it keeps me grounded." Who are any of these people, the faculty I mean? An officer for the Federal Bureau of Investigation said they're better than me. At least we may call some advisors. Klosterman's essay about The Sims sold me on Apple's game though not a console is he interested in hashing it out? In Alpes-Maritimes a summer boarding school for teenagers charged with learning French whose decor remains courtesy of the multidisciplinary artist Jean Cocteau but was it by commission from the other Jean, Moreau? Le Centre organized excursions on the water and to the perfume fabricators in Grasse, my ex-husband's birthplace whom I met years later in Paris. Known as Parfumerie Fragonard, a name borrowed from Rococo painter Jean-Honoré whose La Liseuse belonged to the King's mistress after Louis XV's death. Assured of a Dutch influence on his work, scholars believe Fragonard probably even traveled to Holland. Though the Genevese influence or model for his celebrated libertinism was installed in Amsterdam during Victoriana curators indicate that our painter Jean-Etienne Liotard "took it to Versailles in 1748 to advertise his skills as a pastellist to the French court" decades before Fragonard's composition. Drawn from a family sitting in 1746, it was repeated in 1755 with Susanna Campbell, maternally associated with Scottish military, with an inscription identifying Liotard as "an Italian artist." Their theme exploded in popularity over continuing decades with La Liseuses made by Henri Fantin-Latour (1861), Aimé Jules Dalou (1873), Henri de Toulouse-Lautrec (1889), Théodore Roussel (1890-94), and Henri Matisse (1895) such that it is now a meme. After the Second World War, one Jean François Lyotard born in Versailles (per Wikipedia) theorized postmodernism as a "language game." Popularizations of French on university campuses included exhaustive discussions of psychoanalysis via Jacques Lacan's *écrits*, whose meditations are translated to be about "lack" whereas he uses the word manque. To express "I miss you" in French one says "tu me manque," you are missing from me. Yes Vanya brought me to the East Coast chapel burying Scottish naval officer for the United States (1775-1787) &

Russia John Paul Jones in repulse of sovereignty. On Goodreads it was an avatar reproducing Fragonard contemporary albeit jacobin Jacques-Louis David's aunt reading in 1769 held by Chicago's Art Institute from username Tina that boded promising in my research on *Art of The Deal*, whose early November 2016 reviews delight at transcription of "voice." Unlike dozens, the_bean replied to share how Amazon revoked {her} reviewing privileges. Also studying herbalism, since we messaged Tina shelved *Jonathan Livingston Seagull* by Richard Bach, which spiders recently sealed shut here too. Posting a review for Donald J. Trump's cover, Tina assigned three stars tagged financial jotting "Some may dislike him but he's got some sound advice" it was 15 February 2008; Nounou Bazelais had opened this conversation a year previous almost exactly.

You have just finished reading the sequel to <a href="https://www.lulu.com/shop/vira-uabpodu/replicate-this/ebook/product-w4rjjrk.html">Replicate This</a>, a short-read published February 2025 that is also accessible for $2.99. How do you feel? I hope you liked it, literally and not only like that. Personally feeling flattered to have your attention this way because there are crueler avenues, ask around) Meanwhile you are <a href="https://discord.gg/kJyJfVyvEW">invited</a> to learn more about the project on my _{discord} channel using the linked invite which has no user limits or expiration dates, in contradistinction to perishables which I'd rather take off a tree or uproot than buy from this bookseller. Matching Googlers Larry Page and Sergey Brin, my papa's named Сергей; he labels his contribution Computer Science (CS) because his parents were chemical engineers but his degrees were taken in the fine arts. It's that CS trends through its amalgamation/consolidation of novel disciplines like cognitive science though its artistic or humanistic praxis is [[BASIC]]. Starkly splitting disciplines along a post-hierarchical apprehension of science and art has been thought a Renaissance phenomenon though it's my understanding 'schism' was religious fanaticism. Further I wouldn't say Turing is inconsistent with compromises on personal computation towards redistribution etc et era <i>conferatur</i> Hayles, Katherine: <u>How We Became Posthuman: Virtual Bodies in Cybernetics, Literature, and Informatics</u> (2000). Some utter words like "beautiful language" in describing Javascript though it's actually terminal commands using standard English, you know? Except that is what I would prefer barking at a Windsor Tussaud during vegan high tea instead of quoting from peer-review if forced to cosplay so. Thus overturned are delicate sensibilities, the error is not but mobility don't sell out want. In 2020 what I found was an {opun} command within spreadsheets generated by a Natural Language Processor that required human labor to expand. How it clicked with shortcuts like ⌘-O mattered because of a Russian joke someone told me in childhood: "do you love tomatoes?," a literal translation though usage is free with <i>like</i> and <i>love</i> such. | There are two ways of translating the 'punchline,' <i>Есть люблю, но так не очен</i>, but in ignorance of declension: "To eat? Yes. But otherwise, not really" | "There is love, but not really." Only the first definition is grammatically correct; the second matters too. </div>

www.ingramcontent.com/pod-product-compliance
Lightning Source LLC
LaVergne TN
LVHW070048070526
838201LV00036B/362